THE LORDSHIP OF THE
HOLY GHOST

by AP Azariah Hasula

Copyright © 2024 by Todd Laulusa

All rights reserved. No part of this publication may be reproduced, distributed, or transmitted in any form or by any means, including photocopying, recording, or other electronic or mechanical methods, without the prior written permission of the publisher, except in the case of brief quotations embodied in critical reviews and certain other noncommercial uses permitted by copyright law.

For permission requests, write to the publisher, addressed "Attention: Permissions Coordinator," at the address below.

Palm Kingdom
3279 N Treaty Rock Blvd
Post Falls, ID 83854
zelda.mageo@palmkingdom.org
www.palmkingdom.org

Printed in United States

"To my Lord Holy Ghost, for pushing me to go beyond all I could ever ask or think."

TABLE OF CONTENT

Copyright…………………………3

Dedication…………………………..5

Table of Content……………….7

The Preface…………………..10

Holy Ghost in Creation……..15

Ancient Paths, Divine Patterns, and the Holy Ghost…………..21

Jesus and the Holy Ghost…..31

Make Way for Holy Ghost……44

Holy Ghost: Hear Him………..52

Final Thoughts…………………61

Book Review…………………,..65

THE PREFACE

When Jesus returns, will you be ready? If God is the author and finisher of faith, then how will He finish your salvation, which He started? The answer to these questions is found in the Lordship of the Holy Ghost. In fact, God communicates this truth through a parable, which is a short story with a lesson.

In the book of Matthew, Jesus prophesied the spiritual condition of many believers before His return. This prophecy is found in the parable known as "The Ten Virgins" (Mat 25:1-13). In this parable, the determining factor between those who were wise and those who were foolish was the possession of oil for their lamps. The scriptures portray oil and fire as symbols commonly associated with the Holy Ghost. This is notably seen in the Tabernacle of Moses, where, in the Holy Place, stood a seven-branched lamp full of oil. Its flames were to never go out, symbolizing the seven torches before the throne of God in heaven, representing the seven Spirits of God (Exo 25:37, Rev 4:5, Isa 11:2).

Looking at this parable, several outcomes arose from the foolish virgins' decision to take no oil:

1. Their fire was going out (Mat 25:8).

2. They had to depend on others to supply oil (Mat 25:9).

3. They missed the arrival of the bridegroom (Mat 25:10).

4. They were denied entrance to the marriage feast by the bridegroom (Mat 25:11-12).

Considering these outcomes, it's remarkable how they all stemmed from the absence of one crucial component. All these hardships could have been avoided if the foolish virgins had taken oil with their lamps.

The same analogy applies to the Church. Many hardships would be avoided if we would allow the Holy Ghost to have His way. A Church without the Holy Ghost is like a lamp without oil. Such a Church, refusing the Lordship of the Holy Ghost, will face outcomes similar to those of the foolish virgins: they will begin to burn out, depend on others resources, miss the coming of the Lord Jesus, and be denied access to heaven by the Lord Jesus Himself. It's time for us to align with the wise by yielding to the movement of the Holy Ghost. Throughout the scriptures, it has always been the Father and the Son's plan for the

Church to be under the Lordship of the Holy Ghost. Therefore, let us take a journey through the Bible and learn more about this plan of God.

He is the same from everlasting to everlasting, and there is no shadow of turning or variation with Him (Mal 3:6, Jas 1:17, Rev 1:8). In fact, it is the unchanging character of God that truth is founded on. We are able to receive faith from His Word, because He will not change His mind, lie, or cause confusion about the things He says. His Word is yes and amen (Num 23:19, 1Co 14:33, 2Co 1:20). It is in the light of these truths that we will look to the creation of every believer and see that the Holy Ghost is still doing His part of the creation process today.

The first question that we must answer is, "Are believers a creation of the Lord God?" The answer to this question is a resounding

"Yes". The scriptures declare that He has removed the heart of stone and given us a heart of flesh. They also say that He has placed His Spirit within us. They say that We are a new creation in Christ, and being this new creature is what gives us a right standing before our Holy God (Eze 36:25-27, 2Co 5:17, Gal 6:14-15). Now, if we, as believers, are a new creation of the Lord God, then there must be the work of God the Father, God the Son, and God the Holy Ghost clearly seen in every believer's life, for this process is the truth of creation. Do the scriptures reveal to us the clear truth of the Father, Son, and Holy Ghost's work in a believer? Again, the answer is undoubtedly "Yes". It was the Plan of the Father, which is His love for creation, that sent the Son. It was the Word of the Plan, being the Gospel message of Jesus, that sent the Holy Ghost, and it is the Life of the Plan, which is the leading of the Holy Ghost, that fulfills the Gospel of our salvation (Joh 3:14-16, Joh 16:13-15). This is the creation process of every believer, and without each work of the Godhead Trinity, there is no new creation. Without each of them, nothing could have been made that was made (Rom 8:9, 1Jn 2:23).

As we come to the end of this section, the question that we must answer today would be, "Is the creation process of every believer completed or is it still ongoing?" The scriptures tell us that, while the love of the Father was expressed, which is the Plan, and the message of the Son was given, which is the Word of the Plan, the Holy Ghost is still working to sanctify us wholly and completely, which is the Life of the Plan. He is preserving us for the coming of the Lord Jesus Christ (Gal 4:4-6, 1Th 5:23). Therefore, let us yield to the Lordship of the Holy Ghost, for without each of the Godhead's work being done, there is no creation of anything, including the believer.

CHAPTER 2

Ancient Paths, Divine Patterns, and Holy Ghost

In the Bible, God also communicates to us through seasons and times. In this section, we'll be exploring this truth, in order to reveal our second understanding of the Lordship of the Holy Ghost.

Now, because the Lord God never changes, is faithful, and is true, we are able to find His ways paved in the pages of scripture. These ways can also be seen as ancient paths or divine patterns. The Lord God sets these paths or patterns so that you and I may follow after Him, see, and catch His eternal plan. These ways can be seen in the scriptures through the lifestyle of people and the instructions of God. They can also be found in the Lord's dealings with men through a historical narrative (Jer 6:16, Isa 30:21, Song 1:7-8, Col 2:6). In this section, we will observe these ancient paths or divine patterns to find the Holy Ghost's place in the plan of salvation.

The first path or pattern we will consider is found in the deliverance of the people of Israel out of Egypt and into the promised land. Now, when it comes to this account, we know that it is an ancient path or divine pattern because it is repeated in the times of Jesus and the acts of His apostles. In the Exodus, we see three main elements:

1. God sends forth a deliverer.

2. The lamb's blood averts death.

3. The pillar of cloud and fire is given to lead and guide.

The Lord God begins His plan of delivering Israel or the salvation of Israel by sending Moses. Moses went forth with a message that was to be validated by signs following.

Then, to finally break the hold of Pharaoh and the Egyptians, the Lord God sends a plague of death that can only be averted by the blood of a lamb without blemish. Lastly, to bring the people of Israel into the promised land, He guides them with a pillar of cloud and fire (Exo 3:1-10, Exo 12:7-13, Exo 13:21-22). Now, if these things sound familiar to you, it is due to it being an ancient path or divine pattern of God, for the Lord does the same thing to save or deliver the world out of sin. The Father sends forth His Son with a message that is validated by signs following. Then, to break the wages of sin, which is death, Jesus, the Lamb of God, sheds His blood on the cross. Finally, in the book of Acts, the Holy Ghost is given to guide and lead the believers, as a sound comes down from the sky where clouds gather, and tongues of fire rest on each of those who were gathered in the upper room (John 1:15-18, Mark 15:24-26, Acts 2:1-3). In the times of the Exodus, the pillar of cloud and fire guided them until the people of Israel crossed over into the promised land as a whole. This also reveals to us when the work of the Lord Holy Ghost will end. He will continue to lead and guide until all of the redeemed are in the arms of Jesus. This also shows us that the Lord God's plan of salvation is not complete until the Lord Holy Ghost has completed His work (1 Thessalonians 5:19-23).

The last ancient path or divine pattern that we will look at are three feasts that the Lord God establishes in the Old Testament as He renews His covenant with the people of Israel. These feasts are:

1. The Feast of Passover

2. The Feast of Weeks or Pentecost

3. The Feast of Harvest

What is amazing about these three feasts are their meanings, aside from the awesome truth of them being a path or pattern. The Passover is a feast that reminds the people of Israel how God caused the angel of death to pass over them. Again, this was made possible through the spilling of the blood of a lamb without blemish. Starting directly after and fifty days from the feast of Passover, the Lord God institutes the Feast of Weeks or Pentecost. This feast was a celebration of first fruits. In this feast, the Israelites were to bring to the Lord the first fruits of the harvest. The third feast was held at the end of the year, which is the Feast of Harvest. It was a joyous time of bringing in the harvest (Exo 12:14-27, Exo 23:15-16). Did you catch the ancient path or divine pattern seen in these three feasts? Let us go on into the New Testament and reveal how these three feasts are repeated. The Passover Feast is seen in the death of our Lord Jesus, as he shed His blood for the forgiveness of sin. The second feast, which is the Feast of

Weeks or Pentecost, is seen in the book of Acts when the first fruits of the Church were birthed by the sending of the Holy Ghost. Lastly, the Feast of Harvest is found in the book of Revelation when the Lord gathers all of those righteous who were left upon the earth while passing His final judgment upon the wicked. This is known as the Day of the Lord. Now, more amazing than finding the similarities of the three feasts in the New Testament is the truth that these are undoubtedly the times that match the feasts. Jesus was crucified on the very day that people slay the lamb for Passover. The birthing of the Church, which is its first fruits, happened on the fiftieth day of the Feast of Weeks or Pentecost. The Lord's Day will happen at the end of the age, which is just like the Feast of Harvest happening at the end of a year. This is surely the Lord God speaking to all His people and revealing His eternal plan of redemption (John 19:30, Acts 2:1, Revelation 14:14-16).

As we close out this understanding of ancient paths or divine patterns, let us consider where we are in the timeline of these paths or patterns. If we have truly seen that which the Lord God is unveiling to us, we would know that we are still being led by the pillar of cloud and fire. We are in between the Feast of Weeks and the Feast of Harvest. Scriptures are clear that it is the Lord Holy Ghost that leads and guides us. The scriptures also declare that it is the Lord Holy Ghost who causes us to bear forth fruit. It is He who will prepare and present us to the Lord Jesus on the day of His return. Therefore, if we are to partake of these ancient paths or divine patterns of the Lord God, then we need to yield to the Lordship of Holy Ghost in order to enter the promised land and celebrate the Feast of Harvest (John 16:13, Galatians 5:22-25, 1 Thessalonians 5:19-23).

CHAPTER 3

Jesus and the Holy Ghost

One of the greatest ways that God communicates to us, in the Bible, is by a living example. He uses the life of his servants, in order to convey truth. This is how we will receive our third understanding of the Lordship of the Holy Ghost.

Now, when it comes to how a Christian should walk in this journey of salvation, the scriptures are very clear. Jesus is our example to follow. In fact, He Himself declared this when Thomas, one of His disciples, asked Him, "How will we go where you are going, when we don't know the way?" Jesus answered him, "I AM the way and the truth and the life." In the Greek, Jesus' statement holds many definite conclusions. The way means the traveler's road. The truth means that which is consistent throughout time, no matter what. The life means the thing which possesses or owns vitality. In short, Jesus is saying that His character is the only path to travel, no matter the day or age we might be in. His way of living is proven righteous before God, for it alone is full of the life that only God can give (John 14: 5-6). Even in the times of the Apostle Paul, as he was dealing with the issues of Jewish and Gentile believers, he tells them that the way they can know how to live with each other is by imitating him, as he imitates Jesus. The word imitate means to follow by copying. Paul was stating that Jesus is the way, the truth, and the life to living with others (1 Corinthians 11:1).

Now, when it comes to the Holy Ghost, what did Jesus do? How did He interact with the Holy Ghost during His earthly ministry? Since Jesus is the way, the truth, and the life that we, as believers, should follow, understanding the answers to these questions is crucial to our interactions with the Holy Ghost.

The first thing we see Jesus doing with the Holy Ghost is being born of Him. The scriptures tell us that Mary asked the angel how she would give birth to the Christ, so the angel answered that the Holy Ghost would come upon her and the power of the Most High shall overshadow her (Luke 1: 34-35). Later, when Joseph thought to divorce Mary secretly in order to save her from shame, an angel told him not to be afraid to take Mary as his wife, for the child she carries is of the Holy Ghost (Matthew 1:19-20). Again, this proves that Jesus was born of the Holy Ghost.

Not only that, but Jesus also taught that we all must be born of the Holy Ghost. There was a time when a teacher of Israel named

Nicodemus approached Jesus in the night. He desired to understand what exactly Jesus' mission was and who Jesus might be. Immediately, Jesus began to talk about being born again. Puzzled, Nicodemus struggled to understand what Jesus was getting at. Jesus then told him that he must be born of water and the Spirit. We must see, in this section of scripture, that Nicodemus sought to understand what Jesus' mission was and who Jesus might truly be, but Jesus was telling him that it can't be done, until Nicodemus is born of the Spirit, for spiritual things are spiritually understood. Only those who are born of the Spirit can know spiritual things. Jesus tells him, "That which is flesh is flesh, but that which is Spirit is spirit." Then He says, "You must be born again." (John 3:3-7) The same is for us today. We must be born of the Spirit, if we are to truly understand spiritual things. Jesus was born of the Holy Ghost. Therefore, we must follow the way, the truth, and the life.

The second thing that we find Jesus doing with the Holy Ghost is being baptized or filled by Him. In the scriptures, we find Jesus, after coming up out of the water, prayed, and the Holy Ghost descended on Him, in the form of a dove. Later on, in Luke 4:1, we see, in a clearer way, what exactly happened between Jesus and the Holy Ghost, as the verse reveals to us that Jesus was full of the Holy Ghost (Luke 3:21-22).

This is also something Jesus taught, for when Jesus was ready to leave the earth, He gathers His disciples and tells them to wait in Jerusalem, until they are baptized in or filled with the Holy Ghost. He proclaims that only then will they be able to be His witnesses. Even after all that the disciples had experienced with Him, Jesus still tells them not to leave Jerusalem until they are baptized in the Holy Ghost (Acts 1:4-5). Jesus prayed, and was baptized, and filled with the Holy Ghost. Therefore, we must follow the way, the truth, and the life.

The third thing we find Jesus doing with the Holy Ghost is being led by Him. After being baptized and filled, the Holy Ghost leads

Jesus into the wilderness in order to face off against Satan (Luke 4:1).

Now, we find a similar battle and truth being spoken about by the Apostle Paul, as he addresses issues in the Galatian churches. Lies of the enemy, through false teachings, have corrupted the fellowship of the saints in Galatia, and these deceptions are tempting them to turn from fully trusting in Jesus for their salvation. Therefore, the Apostle tells them to be led by the Holy Ghost, and they will not give in to the lusts of the flesh. This is the exact thing that Jesus did, in order to defeat the enemy's lies in the wilderness. Being led by the Holy Ghost destroys the works of the flesh (Galatians 5:16-17, Galatians 5:24-25).

Jesus was led by the Holy Ghost. Therefore, we should follow the way, the truth, and the life.

The fourth thing that we find Jesus doing with the Holy Ghost is being powered by Him. After handing Satan the first of many defeats, the scriptures tell us that Jesus comes out of the wilderness in the power of the Holy Ghost. This power of the Holy Ghost caused Jesus' fame to spread quickly throughout the regions (Luke 4:14).

As the Apostle Paul writes to the believers in Corinth, they are struggling to understand who the source of power is. They began to place emphasis and popularity on the outward display of flesh, instead of the unseen river of the Holy Ghost that flows out from within. This led the church of Corinth down a path of carnality and made them ignorant of the spiritual. Paul fixes this issue by fixing their focus back upon the Holy Ghost's power as the source of all influence, and off of the efforts of the arm of flesh (1 Corinthians 12:4-7). Now, this is a lesson that we must never forget. The fame or influence of the Church should never be on anything else but the power and might of the Holy Ghost. Jesus' movement and fame came from the power of the Holy Ghost. Therefore, we must follow the way, the truth, and the life.

The final thing that we find Jesus doing with the Holy Ghost is being anointed by Him. After coming out of the wilderness in the power of the Holy Ghost, Jesus attends the synagogue. There, the scroll of Isaiah was handed to Him, and He begins to read where the prophet declares that the Spirit of the Lord will anoint the Christ. Then, handing the scroll back to the attendant, He sits down and says, "Today, this scripture is fulfilled" (Luke 4:17-21). The truth of the anointing ceremony is that it symbolizes a choosing. It means that this person is the individual chosen by God to do a certain task. It does not mean power or powerful. The person who has been anointed can receive power due to them being chosen or anointed, but the anointing is a declaration of choice rather than the endowment of power. Remember, Jesus received power from the Holy Ghost before He was anointed or chosen by the Holy Ghost.

Now, the same can be said about the Apostle Paul. He was already receiving visions of the Lord and being taught by Him before he was separated or anointed for the work of an Apostle to the Gentiles. In fact, Paul was in the middle of ministering to the church of Antioch, together with others, when the Holy Ghost chose or anointed him and Barnabas for a task (Acts 13:2-4). If Jesus was anointed or chosen by the Holy Ghost, not to mention everyone else in the scriptures, then we must also follow the way, the truth, and the life.

This is Jesus and the Holy Ghost. These are the things that He, who is the way, the truth, and the life, has done with the Holy Ghost. Therefore, if Jesus is the only path to travel, the sole matter that will never change, and the thing that possesses vitality alone, then we must see the interactions that He had with the Holy Ghost and receive them as our own. If Jesus was born, filled, led, powered, and anointed by the Holy Ghost, which is the Holy Ghost having His way in Jesus, then we should also allow the Lordship of the Holy Ghost to move in us.

CHAPTER 4

Make Way for the Holy Ghost

The most commonly known way that God communicates to us, in the Bible, is through a spoken truth, which can also be known as a "God said". These are truths that are stated clearly through words. We will be looking at spoken truths, this time, in order to grasp our fourth understanding of the Lordship of the Holy Ghost.

Now, as John the Baptist was baptizing in the River Jordan, some of the religious leaders also came to be baptized. Seeing them, John tells them to make sure that they are sincere, for there is another coming who is greater than he. He will baptize with the Holy Ghost and fire. John was referring to Jesus (Mat 3:11). When we look to the words that John spoke about Jesus, he was saying that Jesus is greater than him in every way. He said that Jesus' work is more important than his. He said that Jesus Himself is better in every way than him. In fact, if we go deeper into the meaning of words, the word "coming" means to take over or replace. These deeper meanings are found in the original Greek text. We can also find this very understanding of the word "coming", as we move further on into John's ministry. There came a time when both John and the disciples of Jesus were baptizing in the River Jordan, and John's disciples began to complain how everyone was going to Jesus' disciples to be baptized. John responded with the words, "I must decrease and He must increase." (Joh 3:29-30) This is a spoken truth or a "God said". As the scriptures teach, there cannot be two masters. It cannot be John and Jesus baptizing in the River Jordan. Someone has to decrease, in order for the other to increase. In the case of John and Jesus, it was John that had to make way for Jesus, for Jesus' ministry was better in every way.

Now, let us also consider the prophetic words of John the Baptist. He declared that Jesus would come and baptize in the Holy Ghost and fire. This means that there would come a time when Jesus also had to make way for another. This "another" is the Holy Ghost. Just like in the case of John having to make way for Jesus near the end of his ministry, so the same is said for Jesus. It was near the end of His mission that He began to speak of the "coming" of the Holy Ghost. Jesus tells His disciples that they would not be orphaned, for the Father would send "another" Helper. Someone who would remind them of Jesus' teachings and lead them into deeper truths (Joh 14:16-18 , Joh 14:25-26). It is simply amazing, when we are able to consider the similarities of John making way for Jesus and Jesus making way for the Holy Ghost. John spoke of another "coming" and so did Jesus. John said that the one that is "coming" is better in every way and so did Jesus. Wait... Whaa...

I know what you're thinking. Did Jesus really say that? Well, the answer is yes. Let us consider the words of Jesus in Joh 16:7.

"Nevertheless I tell you the truth: It is to your advantage that I go away, for if I do not go away, the Helper won't come to you. But if I go, I will send him to you."

Jesus said "I tell you the truth." This means that the statement Jesus is about to make is unquestionably true and not a lie. The word "truth" in this verse means objectively true in every way.

Jesus then says, "It is to your advantage that I go away." The word "advantage" means profitable. It is the picture of something being taken further than where it is currently.

Just like John the Baptist told his disciples that Jesus will take people further than he has, so Jesus is saying, to His disciples, that the Holy Ghost will take them further than He has. This is the "truth", for Jesus' ministry was to set men free from sin, but the Holy Ghost's ministry is to keep men free from sin. How is this possible? The answer is through the Lordship of the Holy Ghost, for the spoken truth declares:

"Now the Lord is the Spirit, and where the Spirit of the Lord is, there is "liberty"

(2Co 3:17)

This spoken truth or "God said" is telling us that, while Jesus set us free from sin, it is the Holy Ghost who will give us the power to stay free from sin. The Apostle Paul is also telling us that "Now" the "Lord" is the "Spirit". What he means is that the one who will give us the power of the New Covenant in Christ is the Holy Ghost, and the Holy Ghost will do this through His "Lordship". The word "Lord" means owner, master, or the one who has the power to decide. Therefore, if we are to go further into our salvation and partake of the power of the new covenant in Christ, which is to stay free from sin, then we must surrender to the Lordship of the Holy Ghost.

CHAPTER 5

Holy Ghost: Hear Him

As we come to the end of our journey through the Bible, in order to fully understand the Lordship of the Holy Ghost, I want us to consider the concept of "last words". Whenever someone is about to leave, they always pick and choose their final words very carefully. God communicates to us that those who understand the book of Revelation, which is the "last words" of the Bible, are blessed. The book of Revelation unveils to us something that Jesus commands, which will bring us to our final understanding of the Lordship of the Holy Ghost, so hold on one last time, as we take our closing journey through the Bible.

In the book of Genesis, we learn how our God created everything. How He took that which was formless, empty, and dark, and brought it to have purpose, be full, and bright. The Lord God did all these things with His words (Gen 1:1-3). As we look to the New Testament, we learn, when Satan tried to get Jesus to bring life to Himself by using His powers to turn stones into bread, Jesus answered, "Man does not live by bread alone, but by every word that proceeds from the mouth of God." (Mat 4:4) Now, if God creates all things with His words and Jesus says that life comes from the words that proceed out of the mouth of God, then one of the most important spiritual senses that the Lord God has given to us, as believers, is the spiritual sense of hearing. This spiritual sense is similar to our physical hearing, but it pertains to the things that are spiritual. Jesus would often say, after giving a message from God, "Let those who have ears, hear." Everyone He spoke to had physical ears and were able to hear, yet He still said these words to them. This shows us that Jesus wasn't referring to the physical ear, but a spiritual one (Mat 11:14-15). The word hear, in the Old and the New Testament, can mean the physical ability to hear, but it can also mean to understand, perceive, consider, listen, obey, and pay attention. These are the more spiritual meanings of the word hear.

In the book of Deuteronomy, Moses is preparing the Israelites, to cross over, into the promised land. They will be led by Joshua, his successor, for the Lord God has refused Moses to enter in. Now, in order to assure the blessings of the Lord upon His people, Moses commands that they hear what he is about to tell them (Deu 6:3-4). Remember that the word hear doesn't only mean to hear physically. We also learned, at the beginning of this article, that life comes from every word that proceeds out of the mouth of God. Therefore, Moses is not telling them to simply hear what he is about to say, but he is telling them to understand, perceive, and consider. Moses knows that spiritual hearing is key to receiving the blessings of God.

As the Israelites conquested Canaan, received the promised land, built their nation, went into several times of exile, and received back their land, they began to truly see how the blessings of the Lord God were connected to hearing the words of God through Moses and the prophets. Therefore, in the times of Jesus our Lord, they have become very fixed on hearing only Moses and the prophets, but is that what Moses and the prophets were saying? Were they saying, "Only hear us," or were they saying, "Hear the Lord God,"? The depths of this fixation to only hear Moses and the prophets was so embedded in the Israelites that even the three main disciples of Jesus honored it, for there was a time when Moses and Elijah appeared before them. They were so astonished that Peter suggested to build a tent for Jesus, Moses, and Elijah, but before Peter could finish all that he wanted to say, a cloud covered them and the voice of the Father said, "This is My Son. Hear Him." Why did the Father tell the three to hear Jesus? It was due to the fact that the Father knew their hearts and why they wanted to set up tents for Moses and Elijah. They wanted to hear their words, but the Father commanded them to hear Jesus. Mat 17:1-5 This means that the words of the Lord God, in the Old Testament, came through Moses and the prophets, but in the days of Jesus, the words of God were coming through Him.

A great question to ask at this time would be, "Who is speaking the words of God now?" The answer to this question can be found in the book of Revelation. At the writing of this letter, John the beloved is exiled to the Island of Patmos, while the persecution of believers was spreading throughout the Roman Empire. Being in the Spirit, on the Lord's day, John was given a revelation of things to come. Now, a portion of this letter was written to encourage the churches to overcome, and it is in this section of the book of Revelation that we find who to yield our spiritual sense of hearing to. Seven times, Jesus tells the churches to hear the Holy Ghost. He says, "He who has an ear. Let him hear what the

Spirit says to the churches." Just like the Father told the three disciples, who were looking at Moses and Elijah, to hear Jesus, so the resurrected Savior is telling the churches, who are looking to Him, to hear the Holy Ghost (Rev 2:7 , Rev 2:11 , Rev 2:17 , Rev 2:29 , Rev 3:6 , Rev 3:13 , Rev 3:22).

The churches are being persecuted, and Jesus commands, "Hear the Holy Ghost." They are looking to Him for answers, and He commands, "Hear the Holy Ghost." They are feeling formless, empty, and in the dark, just as the earth was in the beginning, and Jesus commands, "Hear the Holy Ghost." They are in need of life, which are the words that proceeds out of the mouth of God, and

Jesus commands, "Hear the Holy Ghost." The one who has the words to create, give life, bless, and help in times of persecution, in this day and age, is the Holy Ghost. Again, just as the Father first spoke through Moses and the prophets, and later through Jesus, so now, Jesus is saying, "This is My Holy Spirit. Hear Him." We must take our spiritual sense of hearing and yield it to the Lordship of the Holy Ghost, if we are to find the life and creative power of the Lord God moving in us.

FINAL THOUGHTS

It is my prayer, as an Apostle, that you were able to gain all that the Lord Holy Ghost has designed for you to receive. As His servant, it is my job to be a good steward over the mysteries of God (1Co. 4:1). I pray that the Lord Holy Ghost has truly opened your eyes to see this mystery of the Kingdom, and that you now know the power found in the Lordship of the Holy Ghost. There are so many other things that the Holy Ghost desires to show and teach us, but we must first receive Him as Lord of our lives today. Remember, the Holy Ghost is not Lord, in order to set you free from sin, for that is the

Lordship of Jesus. The Holy Ghost is Lord, in order to keep you free from sin. The scriptures say, "If we live by the flesh, we will die, but if by the Spirit, we put to death the deeds of the body, we will live, for as many as are led of the Spirit are the sons of GOd (Rom.8: 13-14).

Would you pray with me? Would you give me the honor in leading you into the Lordship of the Holy Ghost? Please pray these words, and I believe that when we are done praying, you will know and experience everything that was revealed in this book and more. Let's pray:

Father, we thank You for loving us so much that you sent your Son. Jesus, we thank you for also loving us so much that you came and died, in order to show us the love of the Father, by setting us free from sin, but God your love didn't end there. You went further and sent us the Holy Ghost, so that we could live a life that is free from sin. You showed us, through this book, that it is through the Lordship of the Holy Ghost that we will walk in power and make it to the coming of Jesus. Therefore, we surrender to You Holy Ghost. Come and be our Lord and prepare us for the coming of Jesus. Come and have Your way and move in and through us. Come and glorify the name of the Father and the Son, in our lives. We receive Your Lordship Holy Ghost. In the mighty name of Jesus. Amen.

Now build your relationship with the Lord Holy Ghost. Talk to Him, and He will talk to you. Ask of Him, and you will receive from Him. Everything that the disciples did with the Lord Jesus, when he was on the earth, do these things with the Lord Holy Ghost, for He is with us, now, on this earth.

As an Apostle, I now release every blessing that the Lord Holy Ghost has desired for you to have. May you be used of the Lord Holy Ghost to do mighty things that no eye has seen, no ear has heard, and no heart has ever conceived. May the blessings of our Lord God overtake you. In Jesus name. Amen.

BOOK REVIEW

Unlock the Power of Your Voice

Dear Valued Reader,

You've embarked on a literary adventure within the pages of our book, and now, we invite you to take the next thrilling step – sharing your experience with fellow readers on Amazon!

Your voice holds immense power, and your unique perspective can guide others into the captivating topical we've crafted. Whether the study moved your heart or left you with lingering thoughts, your review is a beacon for those yet to discover the revelation.

Posting a review is simple and only takes a few moments, but its impact resonates far beyond. Your words become a testament, guiding potential readers and igniting the curiosity of those seeking their next literary escape.

Be a part of the literary conversation. Your review is not just a reflection of your experience; it's a gift to the author and a compass for future readers.

Ready to make a difference? Head to Amazon, find our book, and let the world hear your voice. Your contribution is more than a review; it's an integral part of the literary journey we're on together.

Thank you for being a cherished part of our community. Your thoughts matter, and your review is a beacon in the vast realm of books.

Happy reviewing!

AP Azariah Hasula & The Lordship of the Holy Ghost Team

Made in United States
Orlando, FL
04 February 2024